BUGS

CRICKETS

By William Anthony

KidHaven PUBLISHING

Published in 2022 by
KidHaven Publishing, an Imprint of Greenhaven Publishing, LLC
353 3rd Avenue
Suite 255
New York, NY 10010

Edited by: John Wood
Designed by: Amy Li

Cataloging-in-Publication Data

Names: Anthony, William.
Title: Crickets / William Anthony.
Description: New York : KidHaven Publishing, 2022. | Series: Bugs | Includes glossary and index.
Identifiers: ISBN 9781534537668 (pbk.) | ISBN 9781534537682 (library bound) | ISBN 9781534537675 (6 pack) | ISBN 9781534537699 (ebook)
Subjects: LCSH: Crickets--Juvenile literature.
Classification: LCC QL508.G8 2022 | DDC 595.7'26--dc23

Printed in the United States of America

CPSIA compliance information: Batch #CSKH22: For further information contact Greenhaven Publishing LLC, New York, New York at 1-844-317-7404.

Please visit our website, www.greenhavenpublishing.com. For a free color catalog of all our high-quality books, call toll free 1-844-317-7404 or fax 1-844-317-7405.

PHOTO CREDITS – Images are courtesy of Shutterstock.com. With thanks to Getty Images, Thinkstock Photo and iStockphoto.
Cover – Gabriele Maltini, Karramba Production, Ermak Oksana, ten43, azure1, gluk_digitalt, likhit jansawang, L[illegible] Stone, Melinda Fawver, PetrP, Holger Kirk, Tsekhmister. Recurring Images – ten43, THPStock (paper), Lindsay Stone (header texture), [illegible]Jfin (main background), gluk_digitalt (vector crickets in header), Karramba Productions (parchment), Andrey Eremin, Steve Paint (labels), azure1 (m[illegible]gnifying glass), Ortis, Tsekhmister, domnitsky (page decoration), Ermak Oksana (doodles). P1 – Gabriele Maltini, p2-3 – Eileen Kumpf, p4-5– Patric[illegible]oto, Tianika, Sandra Standbridge (web), p6-7– Anatolich, encikAn, p8-9– MF Photo, Alexander Sviridov, pingphoto17, p10-11– Vichnevskiy Vasi[illegible], Martin Pelanek, IhorSIS, p12-13– Marek Velechovsky, David Dohnal, p14-15– D. Kucharski K. Kucharsk, thatmacroguy, p16-17– Saipudin.Haron, [illegible]IMON.SHIM, Pixelcruiser, p18-19– Evdoha_spb, Kurit afshen, Vibe Images, p20-21– Chayut Thanaponchoochoung, Eileen Kumpf, Tomas Ragina, p[illegible]2-23 – Gelpi, StockSmartStart, Mike McDonald, p24 – Gabriele Maltini

CONTENTS

Words that look like **THIS** can be found in the glossary on page 24.

EXPLORER TRAINING

Hi there! Would you like to be our new bug expert? Our team of explorers is one member short and you could be perfect for the job. First, we'll need to give you some training.

This book will teach you all about crickets. So grab your notepad and your magnifying glass, find a patch of grass, and get ready to jump all around with these incredible insects!

WHAT IS A CRICKET?

Before we start, we need to know about the different parts of a cricket. Crickets are a type of insect. Insects have no backbones and have six legs attached to the middle section of their bodies.

The three main parts of an insect's body are the head, the thorax, and the abdomen.

Crickets have two antennae attached to their heads. These help crickets to **SENSE** the world around them. Most crickets have four wings.

Turn to page 16 to find out about male crickets' special use for their wings.

ADAPTATIONS

Like other bugs, crickets have **ADAPTED** to have many different **FEATURES**. The cricket's back pair of legs are much bigger than the others. Big legs help crickets to make big jumps.

Can you see how much bigger this cricket's back legs are than the others?

A cricket's back legs are so powerful that it can jump up to 30 times its own height! Even though most crickets have wings, they usually jump to move from place to place.

HOME LIFE

Crickets live all over the world in lots of different **HABITATS**. They are known to live in places such as tall trees, long grasses, and tree-filled forests.

Lots of crickets make **BURROWS** underground. Some crickets live underground all the time. Others live underground during the day and explore aboveground at night.

FINDING A FEAST

Crickets are omnivores. An omnivore is an animal that eats both plants and other animals. Crickets will eat almost anything, from other small bugs to leaves and fruit.

If crickets get inside your house, they will even chew on things like paper and cardboard.

Crickets use small **PALPS** to hold and taste their food.

Unlike lots of insects, crickets have mouths that they can bite and chew with. These mouthparts help crickets to easily break up **SOLID** food that other insects can't.

LIFE CYCLE

A female cricket might lay up to 100 eggs at a time.

When crickets are born, they do not look like adult crickets. There are two stages in their life cycle before they become adults. First, each cricket starts out as an egg.

Around two weeks later, the eggs will hatch into tiny creatures called nymphs. Nymphs don't have any wings. Nymphs will then grow into full-sized adults.

SINGING A SONG

Have you ever heard a high-pitched chirping sound outside, late at night? That sound is probably a cricket. Male crickets make the sound to show off to female crickets.

The louder and more powerful the chirp, the more impressive it is to female crickets.

The male cricket sings his chirping song by rubbing his wings together. When the wings rub against each other very quickly, they make a high-pitched sound.

PREDATORS

Just like most bugs, crickets have lots of predators. A predator is an animal that eats another animal. Crickets live in lots of different places, so they have lots of different types of predators.

Frogs are a common predator of crickets.

Crickets don't have much **DEFENSE** against predators. Sometimes they will go silent or try to jump away if there's another animal around.

CRAZY CRICKETS

Lots of bugs have weird features, and crickets do too. When they listen out for each other's chirps, they aren't using ears in their heads. They're using a set of ears on their front legs.

A cricket's ears are placed just below their knees!

You can also tell the **TEMPERATURE** using crickets. That might sound crazy, but crickets chirp much more when it's warm and much less when it's cold. The more chirps you hear, the hotter it is outside.

TIME TO EXPLORE

Well, that's the end of your training. Good news – you've passed! You are now ready to go out and explore the wilderness, armed with your new knowledge. But there's one more thing you'll need before you go...

...your well-earned explorer's badge! Here it is, and it means you are now a cricket expert. Why not make your own badge and wear it with pride? Congratulations, explorer!

GLOSSARY

adapt to change over time to suit the environment

burrow a hole or tunnel dug by an animal

defense something that is used for protection

feature an interesting or important part

habitat the natural home in which animals or plants live

palp a part of an animal attached to the head that helps with touching, tasting, and eating

sense to feel or be aware of

solid firm and stable, not a liquid

temperature how hot or cold something is

INDEX

CONTENTS

Medical care is more accessible, or easy to reach, in some parts of the world than others.